HEALTHY
TO GO

Nutrition

The recipes in this book follow the suggestions of the Dietary Guidelines for Americans and contain whole grains, lean proteins, beans and nuts, fruits and vegetables, and low-fat and low-sodium ingredients, vital for a healthy diet.

The nutrition facts listed use recommended daily allowances *(RDAs)* for comparisons, and any percentages are based on a 2,000 calorie diet *(though your caloric needs may be different)*. Using these numbers will help you attain 100% of nutrients like protein, vitamins, minerals, and fiber by the end of each day without exceeding 100% for things like fat, carbohydrates, cholesterol, and calories. Use the information as an estimate – your actual nutrient values may differ slightly due to the brands you buy or the changes you make while cooking *(like adding salt)*.

Data contained in this book is not intended to be, and does not constitute, medical or health advice. While this data is based on the latest information available to us, we cannot warrant or guarantee the accuracy, adequacy, or recency of it.

Printed in the United States of America
by G&R Publishing Co.

Distributed By:

507 Industrial Street
Waverly, IA 50677

ISBN-13: 978-1-56383-551-3
Item #7128

Healthy Food for People on the Go

Healthy to Go is for busy people like you, who might not always have time for a sit-down meal. Included are ideas for healthy breakfasts, lunches, and snacks to prep ahead of time that are portable, filling, and delicious.

Let Healthy to Go work for you...

✓ Wrap foods individually in foil, plastic wrap, or waxed paper and store in an airtight freezer container. Then reheat just the amount you need.

✓ Label packages with item name and date before storing. In general, frozen items maintain their best quality for 1 to 2 months. Refrigerated items should be used within a week.

✓ Toss a frozen pack into an insulated lunch bag and by lunchtime, it will be mostly thawed and ready to reheat.

✓ Buy "low-sodium," "reduced-sodium," or "no sodium added" products.

✓ Look for "low-fat," "fat-free," "made with 2% milkfat," "reduced-fat," and "light" labels.

✓ Use nutritional "seals of approval" *(such as the Heart Check from the American Heart Association)* to guide you toward healthier ingredients, but then read the labels to verify those nutritional claims.

For delicious, convenient, good-for-you foods that are ready to go when you are, simply...

Prep now. Eat later.

Chicken Burrito Bowls

- 1 C. reduced-sodium black beans, drained & rinsed
- 1 C. cooked brown rice
- 1 tsp. chicken bouillon powder
- 3 T. water
- ¼ tsp. each ground cumin, cayenne pepper, and garlic powder

- 2 C. shredded red cabbage
- 2 C. shredded romaine lettuce
- 1 lb. sliced grilled chicken, cooled
- Sliced green onions
- Salsa and nonfat sour cream, optional

In a microwave-safe bowl, combine beans, rice, bouillon powder, water, and all seasonings. Microwave on high for 1½ minutes or until heated through; stir and let cool.

In each of four individual bowls, layer ½ cup each bean mixture, cabbage, and lettuce. Arrange ¼ of the sliced grilled chicken on top and sprinkle lightly with green onions. Cover and refrigerate for up to 3 days. Before eating, top salad with 2 tablespoons salsa and 1 tablespoon sour cream. ▌

Pack single servings of salsa and sour cream in snack bags for grab-and-go convenience. Cut off a corner and pipe the goodness onto your salad before eating.

Make Ahead

Grill a week's worth of boneless, skinless chicken breasts and store in the refrigerator for up to 1 week so the meat is ready to use in other dishes throughout the week. Slice some chicken to use in mason jar salads *(see pages 6-7)*, chop some to make your favorite chicken salad, or dice and add to brown rice and broccoli for a microwavable lunch. For added flavor, marinate or season the chicken to enhance your recipes.

MASON JAR *Salads*

Pack lunches like these in wide mouth quart-size mason jars and refrigerate for up to 5 days. Layer any ingredients you like, but keep in mind that salads with meat, hard-cooked eggs, or cheese are best

Mexican

Mexican cheese blend

romaine salad mix

black olives

tomatoes

green onion

taco-seasoned chicken

red onion

red bell pepper

green bell pepper

salsa

Use 4 ounces of chicken and go heavy on the veggies and salsa, but light on the cheese to keep this salad under 300 calories. Note that sturdier vegetables are put at the bottom in jar salads.

Italian

Draining canned beans and rinsing them well in cool water reduces the sodium content significantly, but you'll still get all the great protein. Boost flavor in any recipe with fresh herbs like basil.

baby spinach

fresh or roasted red pepper

garbanzo beans *(drained & rinsed)*

fresh mozzarella cheese pearls

fresh basil

tomatoes

red onion

Italian dressing

if eaten within 3 days. Use 2 to 4 tablespoons dressing or salsa for each salad, and when you're ready to eat, turn the jar upside down and shake to disperse. Eat directly from the jar or dump the salad onto a plate. So convenient! ▮

Greek

toasted pine nuts

feta cheese

chopped kale & mixed salad greens

cannellini beans *(drained & rinsed)*

marinated artichokes

kalamata olives

cucumber

grape tomatoes

lemon vinaigrette

To make our lemon vinaigrette, combine 2 T. lemon juice, ½ tsp. lemon zest, ¼ C. olive oil, ¼ tsp. salt, and ⅛ tsp. black pepper in a shaker jar; mix well. This salad is full of protein, fiber, and Vitamins A and K.

Asian

To keep dressing and salad ingredients separate until mealtime, mold a 7" square of parchment paper into a shallow cup on top of the jar. Add dressing and attach lid. Before eating, poke holes in the paper to release dressing.

peanut or sesame-ginger dressing

carrots

Japanese udon noodles *(cooked & cooled)*

shelled edamame *(cooked & cooled)*

yellow bell pepper

green onion

purple cabbage

Nutrition

Makes 12 servings
Serving Size: 1 bar

<u>Amount per serving</u>

Calories	349
Total Carbs	49g (16%)
Total Fat	14g (21%)
Sugars	24g
Protein	9g (19%)

Loaded PB Breakfast Bars

2 eggs

⅔ C. unsweetened applesauce

1 tsp. vanilla

⅔ C. creamy peanut butter *(not reduced-fat)*

½ C. honey

1 C. whole-wheat flour

2 C. cooked & cooled quinoa *(do not pack)*

2 C. quick-cooking oats

⅔ C. sliced almonds

1 tsp. cinnamon

1 tsp. baking soda

2 T. chia seeds

⅔ C. dried sweetened cranberries

½ C. dark chocolate chips

Preheat the oven to 375° and grease a 9 x 13″ baking pan.

Combine the eggs, applesauce, vanilla, peanut butter, and honey in a large bowl and mix well. Add all remaining ingredients and stir until evenly combined. Spread in the prepared pan and bake for 20 minutes or until golden brown and set. Cool and cut into bars. Store in the refrigerator.

To Go: Pack each bar in plastic wrap or separate zippered baggies so they're ready to grab and go anytime. To reduce the calories or satisfy petite appetites, simply cut into smaller pieces. ▮

 Excellent source of fiber! 7g (26%)

Nutrition

Makes 20 servings
Serving Size: 1 burrito

<u>Amount per serving</u>

Calories	255
Total Carbs	24g (8%)
Total Fat	11g (17%)
Protein	16g (31%)
Sodium	554mg (23%)

Breakfast Burritos

2 large baking potatoes, peeled & chopped

2 tsp. canola oil, divided

1 lb. turkey breakfast sausage

½ each green and orange bell pepper, chopped

1 C. chopped onion

12 eggs

½ C. skim milk

¼ tsp. salt

Black pepper to taste

2 C. reduced-fat shredded Mexican cheese blend

20 (8") flour tortillas

Look for "healthier" tortillas made with whole grains and lower carbs, calories, and sodium (240 milligrams or less).

Cook potatoes in boiling water until just tender, about 7 minutes; drain and let cool. Heat 1 teaspoon oil in a large skillet over medium heat. Add the sausage, bell pepper, and onion and cook 6 to 7 minutes, crumbling the meat until just cooked through. Drain and let cool.

In a medium bowl, whisk together eggs, milk, salt, and pepper. In a large skillet over medium heat, add remaining 1 teaspoon oil. Add egg mixture and stir until cooked but still shiny. Remove from heat and let cool.

Combine the sausage and potato mixtures with eggs and divide evenly among tortillas *(approximately ½ cup each)*; sprinkle each with about 1½ tablespoons cheese. Roll up burrito-style and place on a parchment paper-lined cookie sheet. Freeze until solid, about 2 hours. Transfer burritos to an airtight container and freeze for up to 3 months. ∎

To Go

Wrap the burritos individually in foil before freezing so you can grab as many as you want on your way out the door. To reheat, remove the foil and rewrap in a paper towel. Microwave until warmed through, 30 to 60 seconds.

Nutrition

Makes 12 servings
Serving Size: 1 muffin cup

Amount per serving

Calories	95
Total Fat	4g (6%)
Protein	7g (14%)
Sodium	169mg (7%)
Cholesterol	39mg (13%)

Ham & Cheese Cups

Preheat the oven to 350°. Generously coat 12 standard muffin cups with cooking spray.

Mix 2 C. cooked and cooled quinoa, 2 eggs, 2 egg whites, 1 C. shredded zucchini, 1 C. low-fat shredded cheddar cheese, 2 T. grated Parmesan cheese, ½ C. diced ham, ¼ C. chopped fresh parsley, and 2 sliced green onions until well combined. Season with black pepper. Spoon into prepared cups and bake 25 to 30 minutes or until firm and golden brown around edges. Cool 5 minutes, then loosen from pan and remove cups.

Serve warm, or cool completely and refrigerate for up to 4 days. You may flash-freeze them on a cookie sheet until solid and transfer to an airtight container *(or wrap individually)* to store in the freezer. Reheat in the microwave. ∎

Nutrition

Makes 8 servings
Serving Size: 1 popsicle

Amount per serving

Calories	60
Total Carbs	15g (5%)
Sugars	12g
Dietary Fiber	1g (5%)
Vitamin C	27mg (45%)

Strawberry-Cherry Popsicles

In a blender container, combine 2 C. sliced fresh strawberries,
1¼ C. pitted sweet fresh cherries, 3 T. lemon juice, and
¼ C. agave nectar. Blend until smooth. Pour into 3-oz. molds
and freeze until solid. Run mold under water a few seconds
to loosen and remove pop. ▮

Cold, fruity, and sodium-free, with no fat, artificial food colorings, or additives — just pure, healthy refreshment!

Popeye's Mug Pasta

- 2 C. uncooked whole-wheat penne pasta
- 1 tsp. olive oil
- 1 (10 oz.) pkg. frozen chopped spinach, thawed & drained
- 1 (14.5 oz.) can diced Italian tomatoes
- 1 (15 oz.) can reduced-sodium garbanzo beans *(chickpeas)*, drained & rinsed
- 1 C. diced roasted turkey
- 5 T. feta cheese crumbles or Parmesan cheese
- Black pepper to taste

 No microwave available? Heat the pasta before you leave home and put it in a wide mouth thermos.

Cook the pasta to al dente in boiling water according to package directions. Drain, rinse briefly in water, and toss with oil; set aside to cool.

Squeeze out excess moisture from the spinach and fluff with a fork. Divide the spinach, tomatoes *(with juice)*, garbanzos, turkey, cheese, and pasta evenly among five large microwave-safe mugs or other containers *(16 oz. capacity)*. Stir to combine; seal and refrigerate for up to 5 days *(or freeze for longer storage)*.

For lunch, uncover a mug, add 1 tablespoon water, and cover with a paper towel; microwave on high for 60 seconds. Stir and microwave 45 to 60 seconds more or until hot. Let stand about a minute, then season with pepper. ∎

Make Ahead

Fill muffin cups with cooked pasta or spread in a single layer on a parchment paper-lined baking sheet. Flash-freeze about 30 minutes. Store individual portions in freezer bags in the freezer. Freeze leftover pasta sauces in muffin pans, adding mushrooms, onions, or cooked lean meat to some cups for variety. When solid, transfer to freezer bags. For lunch anytime, grab one sauce bag and one pasta bag, thaw, and reheat in the microwave.

Hummus & Veggie Cups

1 lb. sweet potatoes, peeled & sliced

1 (16 oz.) can reduced-sodium garbanzo beans *(chickpeas)*, drained & rinsed

⅓ C. tahini

¼ C. lemon juice

¼ C. olive oil

1 T. chopped chipotle peppers in adobo sauce

1 tsp. ground cumin

¼ tsp. salt

Fresh vegetables for dipping

Cook the sweet potatoes in a saucepan of boiling water for 12 to 15 minutes or until very tender. Drain and let cool. In a food processor, combine sweet potatoes, garbanzos, tahini, lemon juice, oil, chipotle peppers, cumin, and salt. Process until relatively smooth. Cover and chill at least 2 hours.

Wash a variety of vegetables and pat dry; trim to 3″ to 4″ lengths or cut in rounds or florets. Thread some on wooden skewers for easy dipping. Spoon about ¼ cup hummus *(or a favorite low-calorie dip or dressing)* into the bottom of each to-go cup and then add raw veggies. Try bell pepper strips; jicama, carrot, celery, or zucchini sticks; broccoli or cauliflower florets; green beans or pea pods; asparagus spears; cherry or grape tomatoes; radishes; and green onions. ∎

In addition to the protein, low sodium, and low sugar content of hummus, the sweet potato in this recipe adds loads of Vitamin A.

Nutrition

Makes 12 servings
Serving Size: ¼ cup

Amount per serving

Calories	145
Total Carbs	15g (5%)
Total Fat	9g (14%)
Sugars	2 g
Protein	4g (7%)

Lemon-Blueberry Muffins

Preheat the oven to 350°. Grease or line 14 standard muffin cups and set aside.

Stir together 2 C. whole-wheat flour, 1 tsp. baking powder, ½ tsp. baking soda, ¼ tsp. salt, and 2 T. lemon zest. In a large bowl, whisk together 1 T. melted coconut oil *(or butter)*, 2 egg whites, and 2 tsp. vanilla. Stir in ½ C. agave nectar and ½ C. plain nonfat Greek yogurt until smooth. Stir in ¼ C. lemon juice. Alternately add flour mixture and ¼ C. skim milk to egg mixture and stir until just combined. Fold in 1½ C. fresh blueberries. Divide batter among prepared muffin cups and bake for 20 to 22 minutes or until tops feel lightly firm to the touch. Cool 10 minutes before transferring to a cooling rack. If you'd like, wrap muffins separately and freeze for up to 1 month. Thaw before eating or warm up in the microwave. ∎

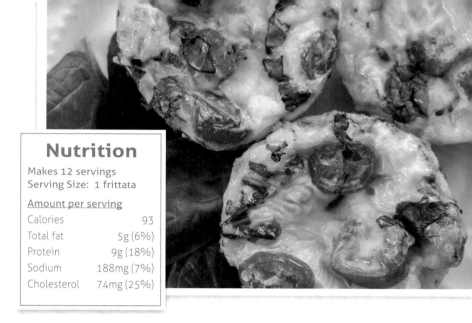

Nutrition

Makes 12 servings
Serving Size: 1 frittata

Amount per serving

Calories	93
Total fat	5g (6%)
Protein	9g (18%)
Sodium	188mg (7%)
Cholesterol	74mg (25%)

Mini Spinach Frittatas

Preheat the oven to 350°. Coat 12 standard muffin cups with cooking spray or use foil-lined paper liners and spray well.

In a skillet, brown 6 lean turkey breakfast sausage links until fully cooked; chop coarsely. Divide the sausage, ½ C. chopped fresh spinach, and ½ C. shredded Colby-Jack cheese evenly among prepared cups. In a bowl, whisk together 4 eggs, 10 egg whites, and ½ C. skim milk; season with black pepper. Pour egg mixture into each cup, filling almost full. Add chopped fresh basil and some halved grape tomatoes, if you'd like. Bake 20 to 22 minutes or until center is firm. Cool 5 minutes, then loosen from pan and remove frittatas.

Serve warm, or wrap each baked, cooled frittata separately and refrigerate for up to 4 days. Reheat in the microwave. ∎

PITA POCKET *Fillings*

Make these main dish fillings and store them in the refrigerator in an airtight container *(or individual baggies)* for 2 to 4 days. For lunch, just

Shrimp Salad

Mix ½ C. light mayonnaise, 2 T. lemon juice, 3 T. reduced-fat sour cream, and ⅛ tsp. black pepper. Gently stir in 12 oz. chopped, ready-to-eat shrimp, 2 C. shredded red cabbage, 1 C. grated carrots, ¼ C. sliced green onions, and ½ C. cashew pieces.

Nutrition

Amount per 1 filled pita half

Calories	356	Total Fat	16g (25%)
Total Carbs	32g (11%)	Protein	25g (49%)

Turkey Salad

Combine ⅓ C. light mayonnaise, ½ tsp. celery seed, and ⅛ tsp. each dried thyme and dried sage. Add 2 C. diced cooked turkey, ½ C. diced celery, ¼ C. sliced green onions, and ⅛ tsp. each salt and black pepper. Top with whole berry cranberry sauce before eating.

Nutrition

Amount per 1 filled pita half

Calories	260	Total Fat	8g (12%)
Total Carbs	23g (8%)	Protein	24g (48%)

spoon some filling into a pita pocket and add a few greens.
Each recipe fills 4 pita halves. ▋

Italian Chicken

Whisk together 2 T. balsamic vinegar, 1 T. chopped sun-dried tomatoes, 1½ T. sun-dried tomato oil, ¼ tsp. black pepper, and ½ tsp. minced garlic. Stir in 2 C. diced grilled chicken breast, 1 C. chopped tomato, ½ C. grated Asiago cheese, and ¼ C. chopped fresh basil.

Nutrition

Amount per 1 filled pita half

Calories	362	Total Fat	17g (26%)
Total Carbs	23g (8%)	Protein	31g (61%)

Tuna Salad

Stir together 1 (12 oz.) can water-pack tuna (drained), ⅓ C. fat-free creamy Italian dressing, ⅓ C. crushed pineapple (drained), and ¼ C. diced red bell pepper.

Nutrition

Amount per 1 filled pita half

Calories	219	Total Fat	2g (2%)
Total Carbs	26g (9%)	Protein	25g (50%)

21

Nutrition

Makes 10 servings
Serving Size: 1 burger

<u>Amount per serving</u>

Calories	246
Total Carbs	38g (13%)
Total Fat	6g (9%)
Protein	10g (21%)
Sodium	268mg (11%)

Sweet Potato Bean Burgers

2 medium sweet potatoes

2 T. olive oil, divided

1 C. old-fashioned oats

1 (15 oz.) can black beans, drained & rinsed

1 C. cooked brown rice

½ C. chopped red onion

½ C. chopped fresh cilantro

1 tsp. minced garlic

1 tsp. ground cumin

1 tsp. paprika

¾ tsp. chili powder

Black pepper to taste

10 whole-grain hamburger buns

Fresh spinach, sliced tomatoes or avocado, salsa, and/or other toppings, optional

Preheat the oven to 425°. Line a rimmed baking sheet with foil. Peel and dice the sweet potatoes and toss with 1½ tablespoons oil. Spread on prepped baking sheet. Roast in the oven for 20 minutes or until tender, stirring after 10 minutes. Let cool.

Meanwhile, process the oats in a food processor until finely ground. Add the beans, rice, onion, and cilantro and pulse until evenly mixed. In a large bowl, coarsely mash the sweet potatoes. Add the oats mixture and all seasonings; mix well. Form into 10 even balls, then flatten into patties. Grill patties on sprayed foil over medium heat, or cook in a skillet on the stovetop with the remaining 1½ teaspoons oil until lightly browned, about 2 minutes on each side. Serve warm on buns with spinach leaves, tomatoes, avocado, salsa, or whatever healthy toppings you like. ▮

Vitamin A and dietary fiber play starring roles in this recipe.

To Go

Wrap the cooked, cooled patties individually in plastic wrap and freeze in an airtight container for up to 2 months. Thaw overnight in the refrigerator; unwrap and reheat in the microwave before eating.

Nutrition

Makes 5 servings
Serving Size: 1 dinner

Amount per serving

Calories	450
Total Carbs	55g (18%)
Total Fat	15g (23%)
Protein	29g (59%)
Sodium	380mg (16%)

Spaghetti & Meatballs

1 lb. lean ground turkey

1 egg, lightly beaten

¼ C. quick-cooking oats

½ tsp. minced garlic

2 T. chopped fresh parsley

½ tsp. black pepper

Pinch of salt

2 T. olive oil, divided

8 oz. uncooked whole-wheat spaghetti

1 (24 oz.) jar low-sodium marinara sauce, divided

1 lb. fresh green beans, trimmed

Parmesan cheese

Mix the turkey, egg, oats, garlic, parsley, pepper, and salt; shape into 10 or 15 meatballs. Heat 1 tablespoon oil in a large skillet and brown the meatballs on all sides until cooked through, 10 to 15 minutes. Remove from heat, drain, and let cool.

Cook the spaghetti to al dente in boiling water according to package directions; drain. Toss with 1 teaspoon oil and half the sauce. In a nonstick skillet, sauté the green beans in remaining 2 teaspoons oil until almost crisp-tender. Divide the pasta among five microwavable freezer containers and top with meatballs and remaining sauce. Divide beans among containers, cover, and freeze.

Thaw before reheating. Remove lid and add 1 tablespoon water. Cover with vented microwave-safe plastic wrap or waxed paper. Microwave on high 4 to 6 minutes or until heated through, stirring several times. Sprinkle lightly with cheese before eating. ∎

 Just like a frozen TV dinner, only better for you.

Spiced Nut Combo

Preheat the oven to 225°. Line a rimmed baking sheet with parchment paper.

In a large bowl, stir together ¼ tsp. ground cloves, ½ tsp. ground ginger, and 1 tsp. each ground cumin, cinnamon, salt, and chili powder. Stir in 2 T. brown sugar and ¼ C. stevia baking blend sweetener *(such as Zing)* or ½ C. sugar. Add 2 egg whites and whisk well for 2 minutes to dissolve sugars. Add 1 C. each raw whole almonds, raw pecans, and raw cashews plus ¾ C. raw pepitas *(shelled pumpkin seeds)* and stir until coated. Spread on the prepped baking sheet and bake for 65 minutes, stirring every 20 minutes. Cool completely and store in an airtight container. ∎

Nutrition

Makes 18 servings
Serving Size: 1 (5 oz.) cup

<u>Amount per serving</u>

Calories	77
Total Carbs	19g (6%)
Sugars	13g
Dietary Fiber	2g (7%)
Vitamin C	33mg (56%)

Frozen Fruit Cups

Drain 1 (15 oz.) can apricot halves and 1 (15 oz.) can mandarin oranges. Coarsely chop the fruit. In a large bowl, combine the apricots, oranges, 1 (8 oz.) can crushed pineapple *(with juice)*, 2 medium diced bananas, and 4 C. any combination of blueberries, chopped strawberries, and chopped mango. Stir in 3 T. lemon juice and 3 C. pineapple-orange juice. Spoon the fruit and juice evenly into 5-oz. disposable cups, small mason jars, or muffin pans, leaving about ¾" headspace at the top. Cover and freeze until firm. *(If using muffin pans, just pop the frozen chunks out and store them in a freezer bag.)*

Remove from the freezer about 1 hour before serving, or toss a frozen one into your lunchbox to thaw by lunchtime. ∎

SMOOTHIES

Place the ingredients for each smoothie into a quart-size freezer bag and freeze for up to 1 month. Freeze fat-free vanilla yogurt in standard muffin cups and add the solid chunks to your ingredient

Strawberry-Kiwi

For each smoothie, put ½ peeled sliced banana, 4 hulled strawberries, ½ peeled sliced kiwi, 2 frozen yogurt chunks, and ⅓ C. pineapple-orange juice in a bag; store in freezer. Blend contents of one partially thawed bag with 2 or 3 ice cubes until smooth.

Nutrition

Amount per serving

Calories	197	Total Carbs	44g (15%)

Vitamin-packed, especially with Vitamin C (172%)

Tropical Mango

For each extra-large smoothie, combine 1 C. chopped mango, ¼ peeled sliced banana, ½ C. unsweetened pineapple juice, 2 frozen yogurt chunks, and 1 T. honey in a bag; store in freezer. Partially thaw contents of one bag, add 2 T. water, and blend until smooth. (Shortcut: Freeze this blended drink in a to-go cup, then let it thaw until slushy.)

Nutrition

Amount per serving

Calories	320	Total Carbs	76g (25%)

Excellent source of Vitamin C & calcium

bags *(or store them in a separate freezer bag for use anytime).* Blend the contents of one bag with other ingredients as directed below. Each bag makes 1 large serving. ▪

Peachy Green

For each smoothie, combine a handful of kale leaves (stems removed), 6 green grapes, 1½ C. sliced peaches, 1 peeled sliced banana, and 1 tsp. ground flaxseed in a bag; store in freezer. Blend one partially thawed bag of ingredients plus ¼ to ½ C. water until smooth.

Nutrition

Amount per serving

Calories	253	Total Carbs	59g (20%)

A good source of calcium, iron, and vitamins A & K

Black 'n' Blueberry

For each smoothie, place ½ C. frozen blackberries, ½ C. frozen blueberries, and 2 T. crushed pineapple in a bag; store in freezer. Dump one partially thawed bag into blender container and add 2 tsp. agave nectar and ¾ C. skim or almond milk; blend until smooth.

Nutrition

Amount per serving

Calories	214	Total Carbs	46g (15%)

A good source of protein & calcium

Nutrition

Makes 8 servings (24 tots)
Serving Size: 3 tots

Amount per serving

Calories	75
Total Fat	2g (3%)
Protein	7g (14%)
Sodium	217mg (9%)
Cholesterol	49mg (16%)

Broccoli Tots

- 1 large head broccoli
- 1 C. shredded Swiss cheese
- ⅓ C. finely chopped onion
- ½ C. panko bread crumbs
- 2 eggs
- ¼ tsp. salt
- ½ tsp. garlic salt
- Black pepper to taste

A tasty source of calcium and Vitamins A, C, and K!

Preheat the oven to 400°. Grease or line 24 mini muffin cups with parchment paper liners and set aside.

Cut the broccoli into florets *(2½ to 3 cups)*. Microwave, steam, or cook broccoli in water until crisp-tender; drain and let cool. Pat dry with paper towels and chop into tiny pieces; transfer to a large bowl. Add the cheese, onion, bread crumbs, eggs, salt, and garlic salt; season with pepper and mix well. Fill prepared cups with the mixture, pressing down and filling to the top. Bake 18 to 20 minutes or until golden brown. Let cool a few minutes before removing from pan. Serve warm. For on-the-run snacking, refrigerate until needed and reheat in the microwave. ▮

Change it Up

Italian Zucchini Tots Drain 2 packed cups grated zucchini on a clean towel and wring out the excess water. Add to a bowl with 2 eggs, ½ cup diced onion, ½ cup shredded smoked Swiss & cheddar cheese, and ½ cup dry Italian-style bread crumbs. Stir in ½ teaspoon each seasoned salt and Italian seasoning. Season with black pepper and mix well. Fill 20 mini muffin cups as directed for Broccoli Tots and bake at 400° for 15 to 18 minutes. Makes 20 tots *(about 7 servings)*.

Though not as rich in vitamins and minerals as Broccoli Tots, you can still enjoy three healthy tots for just under 95 calories.

Sunflower Nut Butter

Toast 3 C. raw unsalted sunflower nuts in a skillet over medium heat for 3 minutes or until lightly browned and fragrant, stirring frequently. Cool completely. Put them in a food processor with ¾ tsp. salt and 1 tsp. sugar. Process about 10 minutes or until the seeds release their oils and mixture is moist-looking *(be patient)*. Drizzle 2 to 4 tsp. olive oil into the mixture and process until smooth and spreadable. Spoon approximately 2 T. nut butter into each small container and serve with carrot and celery sticks, apple slices, whole strawberries, whole-grain crackers, or toasted bread for a snack filled with vitamins and minerals. ∎

Nutrition

Makes 15 servings
Serving Size: 1 cookie

Amount per serving

Calories	167
Total Carbs	25g (8%)
Total Fat	7g (10%)
Sugars	9g
Dietary Fiber	4g (15%)

Blackberry Breakfast Cookies

Preheat the oven to 350°. Line cookie sheets with parchment paper and set aside.

Blend 1¾ C. old-fashioned oats in a food processor for several minutes to get a fine oat flour. Pour into a large bowl and add 2 C. old-fashioned oats, ½ tsp. each baking soda and salt, and ¼ C. ground flaxseed; stir well. Add ½ C. each unsweetened applesauce and mashed banana, ¼ C. plus 2 T. honey, ¼ C. plus 1 T. melted coconut oil, 1 T. lemon zest, and ¼ C. lemon juice; stir until just combined. Fold in 1½ to 2 C. fresh blackberries *(or blueberries)* and let batter rest 10 minutes to thicken.

For each cookie, scoop ¼ C. batter onto prepped cookie sheets and flatten slightly. Bake 15 to 20 minutes or until set on top and lightly browned. Cool completely. Store in the refrigerator or wrap individually and freeze. Thaw before eating. ∎

Mexican Dip Cups

5 (6") corn tortillas

Cooking spray

Coarse salt, optional

1 C. 99% fat-free refried black beans

2 tsp. 40% less-sodium taco seasoning, divided

½ C. fat-free sour cream

½ C. prepared guacamole *(we used Wholly Guacamole)*

½ red bell pepper, chopped

½ C. chunky salsa

⅓ C. reduced-fat shredded Mexican cheese blend

Sliced black olives

¼ C. sliced green onions

1 Roma tomato, chopped

Preheat the oven to 400°. Cut each tortilla into eight wedges and arrange in a single layer on foil-lined baking sheets. Spritz with cooking spray and sprinkle very lightly with salt, if you'd like. Bake 6 to 10 minutes, until crisp and lightly browned. Cool completely.

Mix the beans and 1¼ teaspoons taco seasoning in a small saucepan; cook over medium heat about 5 minutes and let cool. Stir remaining ¾ teaspoon taco seasoning into the sour cream. Divide bean mixture among eight 4- to 5-oz. plastic cups *(about 2 tablespoons each)* and layer evenly with guacamole, bell pepper, sour cream mixture, salsa, cheese, olives, onions, and tomato. Cover cups with foil and refrigerate for up to 3 days. Serve with the chips or raw veggies.

To Go: Divide the chips *(or veggies)* among baggies, then grab a cup of dip and a chip bag for a spicy treat later. ∎

Nutrition

Makes 8 servings
Serving Size: 1 snack cup
                & 5 chips

<u>Amount per serving</u>

Calories	116
Total Carbs	15g (5%)
Total Fat	4g (6%)
Protein	5g (9%)
Sodium	466mg (19%)

Nutrition

Makes 10 servings
Serving Size: 1½ cups

Amount per serving

Calories	196
Total Carbs	23g (8%)
Sugars	6g
Protein	18g (36%)
Sodium	555mg (23%)

Chicken Tortilla Soup

1 T. olive oil

1 lb. boneless, skinless chicken breasts, diced

1¼ tsp. each garlic powder and onion powder

½ tsp. each salt and black pepper

2 jalapeño peppers, seeded & finely diced

1 red bell pepper, diced

2 (32 oz.) cartons unsalted chicken stock *(8 C.)*

1 C. frozen corn

2 (15 oz.) cans diced, "no salt added" tomatoes

1 (15 oz.) can reduced-sodium black beans, drained & rinsed

1 (14 oz.) can yellow hominy, drained & rinsed

1 tsp. ground cumin

1 tsp. chili powder

3 T. lime juice

Heat the oil in a large pot over medium-high heat. Add the chicken, garlic powder, onion powder, salt, and pepper and cook until chicken is no longer pink inside. Stir in jalapeños and bell pepper. Add the stock and all remaining ingredients, stirring until well combined. Bring to a boil and cook about 10 minutes. Keep hot over low heat until serving. Top with a spoonful of guacamole and a few tortilla strips before serving, if you'd like. ▮

The sodium level in this flavorful soup is still under the guidelines for healthy eating (600 milligrams or less per serving in combination foods).

Make Ahead

Cool this soup *(or other broth-based favorites)* and freeze in muffin pans. When solid, set the bottom of pan in warm water just to loosen the soup chunks and transfer them to a labeled freezer container. Freeze for up to 1 month. To prepare, put two frozen chunks into a microwavable dish and seal; by lunchtime, it will be ready to reheat in the microwave.

Nutrition

Makes 10 servings
Serving Size: ½ cup

Amount per serving

Calories	252
Total Carbs	46g (15%)
Total Fat	7g (11%)
Sugars	18g
Dietary Fiber	5g (22%)

Homemade Granola

Preheat the oven to 325°. Line a large rimmed baking sheet with foil and coat with cooking spray. In a large bowl, mix 4 C. old-fashioned oats, 1 C. each Rice Krispies and Kix cereal, ½ C. each flaked coconut and oat bran, ¼ C. each sliced almonds and sunflower nuts, and 3 T. brown sugar; set aside.

In a small saucepan over medium heat, bring ¾ C. pineapple juice and ½ C. apple juice to a boil. Cook until reduced to ⅔ C., about 10 minutes. Stir in ¼ C. honey. Drizzle warm juice over oats mixture, tossing well. Spread on prepped pan and bake 40 minutes or until golden brown, stirring occasionally. Cool slightly. Stir in ¼ C. dried blueberries *(or other dried fruit)* and cool completely. Store in an airtight container. Toss into a bowl with milk, munch as a snack, or use in other recipes like granola bars *(see page 39).* ▌

Nutrition

Makes 16 servings
Serving Size: 1 bar

Amount per serving

Calories	203
Total Carbs	32g (11%)
Total Fat	8g (12%)
Protein	4g (7%)
Dietary Fiber	2g (8%)

Baked Granola Bars

Preheat the oven to 350°. Line a 9 x 13" baking pan with foil and coat with cooking spray. In a large bowl, combine 1⅔ C. Homemade Granola *(see page 38)*, 1 C. each chopped dates and unsweetened raw chip coconut, 3 T. stevia brown sugar baking blend *(or ⅓ C. brown sugar)*, ½ C. whole-wheat flour, and 1 tsp. cinnamon. Stir in 1 (15 oz.) can pinto beans *(drained, rinsed & chopped)* and ½ C. each raisins and chopped walnuts; set aside. In a small bowl, combine ½ C. honey, 3 T. melted coconut oil, 2 T. canola oil, 1 tsp. vanilla, and ⅛ tsp. salt. Pour over granola mixture and stir well. Spread in prepped pan and bake 35 to 40 minutes or until center is firm and edges are browned. Cool completely. Lift from pan and cut into bars. Wrap and freeze for up to 3 months, if you'd like. Healthy carbs for delicious energy! ▮

Nutrition

Makes 5 servings
Serving Size: 1 pizza

<u>Amount per serving</u>

Calories	109
Total Carbs	6g (2%)
Total Fat	6g (9%)
Protein	10g (19%)
Sodium	340mg (14%)

Cauliflower Crust Pizzas

1 small head cauliflower

1½ C. shredded
   mozzarella cheese,
   divided

1 egg

¼ tsp. each dried
   oregano, dried basil,
   garlic powder, and salt

2½ T. pizza sauce

½ C. each diced green
   bell pepper and sliced
   mushrooms

¼ C. diced red onion

White pepper to taste

Chopped fresh basil

Preheat the oven to 425° and line a cookie sheet with greased parchment paper.

Cut cauliflower into florets, discarding most of the stem. Blend florets in a food processor until rice-like and then transfer to a microwave-safe bowl; microwave on high about 4 minutes, until tender. Spread on a clean towel to cool; squeeze out all liquid and dump cauliflower into a bowl. Add 1¼ cups cheese, egg, oregano, basil, garlic powder, and salt; mix well. For each crust, scoop about ½ cup mixture *(packed)* onto prepped cookie sheet and press firmly to flatten. Bake 12 minutes, until bottom begins to brown.

Remove crusts from oven and spread each with about 1½ teaspoons pizza sauce. Sprinkle evenly with bell pepper, mushrooms, red onion, and remaining ¼ cup cheese; season with pepper. Return to oven and bake 3 to 4 minutes longer. Top with fresh basil and let cool 5 minutes before slicing. Serve warm. Pizzas may be refrigerated a day or two and just reheated in the microwave *(1 to 2 minutes)* or a 425° oven *(about 10 minutes)*. Wrap, stack, and freeze for longer storage. Thaw before reheating. ∎

Nutrition

Makes 9 servings
Serving Size: 1½ cups

Amount per serving

Calories	254
Total Fat	6g (9%)
Protein	30g (59%)
Sodium	395mg (17%)
Iron	2mg (12%)

Hearty Chicken Veggie Soup

- 1 whole bone-in chicken breast, skin on *(about 2¼ lbs.)*
- 2 T. olive oil
- 3 celery ribs, sliced
- ¼ C. chopped celery leaves
- 1 onion, chopped
- 5 carrots, peeled & diced
- ½ tsp. salt
- Black pepper to taste
- 1 T. minced garlic

- 1½ tsp. dried thyme
- ¼ C. flour
- 2 (32 oz.) cartons unsalted chicken stock *(8 C.)*
- 1 (14.5 oz.) can low-sodium diced tomatoes
- 1 (15.5 oz.) can low-sodium cannellini beans, drained & rinsed
- 3 C. baby spinach
- 1 T. agave nectar
- 2 T. lemon juice

Preheat the oven to 375°. Line a baking pan with foil and roast the chicken uncovered for 40 to 50 minutes or until skin is light golden brown and chicken is cooked through *(165°)*. When cool enough to handle, shred the meat, discarding skin and bones. Set meat aside *(about 4½ cups)*.

In a large soup pot over medium-high heat, heat the oil. Sauté the celery, celery leaves, onion, and carrots until soft, about 7 minutes. Add salt and season with pepper. Stir in garlic and thyme. While stirring, add flour and cook about 3 minutes. Pour in the stock and tomatoes and bring to a simmer. Add the beans and simmer for 15 minutes, reducing heat as needed. Stir in the chicken and spinach and simmer for 10 minutes longer. Stir in agave and lemon juice. ▪

 Loads of minerals and Vitamins A, B, C, and K!

To Go

Let soup cool and divide it among mason jars or mugs with lids, leaving some headspace at the top. Cover and refrigerate *(or freeze)* until needed. Reheat in the microwave before serving.

For a no-cook hot lunch, fill a thermos with reheated soup in the morning before you leave home.

Oatmeal Packs

Make instant oatmeal packs in a variety of flavors for healthy to-go breakfasts anytime. Just combine the dry ingredients in individual snack bags, seal, and label for prep later. Store bags at room temperature for 1-2 months. **Each recipe makes 1 serving.**

Spiced Apple

For each serving, combine ⅓ C. quick-cooking oats, ¼ C. chopped dried apples *(or pears)*, 2 tsp. brown sugar, ½ tsp. cinnamon, ¼ tsp. ground nutmeg, and a pinch of salt in a bag. *(Add walnuts and/or raisins for more protein and 100 more calories.)*

Nutrition

Amount per serving

Calories	236	Sugars	26g
Total Carbs	52g (17%)	Dietary Fiber	6g (25%)

Tropical

For each serving, combine ⅓ C. quick-cooking oats, 2 T. diced dried mango, 2 T. diced dried pineapple, a few dried banana slices *(broken)*, and 2 T. shredded coconut in a bag.

Nutrition

Amount per serving

Calories	307	Sugars	30g
Total Carbs	54g (18%)	Dietary Fiber	5g (20%)

Strawberry Cream

For each serving, combine ⅓ C. quick-cooking oats, 1 tsp. ground flaxseed, 2 tsp. wheat germ, 2 tsp. nonfat dry milk, 2 tsp. brown sugar, a pinch of salt, and ¼ C. dehydrated strawberries in a bag.

Nutrition

Amount per serving			
Calories	186	Sugars	12g
Total Carbs	34g (11%)	Dietary Fiber	5g (20%)

To prep

Pour one oatmeal pack into a bowl and stir in ⅔ C. boiling water; let stand 4 to 6 minutes to soften. Or to cook in the microwave, combine one oatmeal pack with ¾ C. water or milk in a 12 oz. *(or larger)* microwave-safe bowl; microwave on high about 2 minutes *(watch closely and pause to prevent boil-overs).* Let stand 2 minutes and stir before eating.

Rise & Shine Quesadillas

2 T. olive oil, divided

1 C. diced red onion

½ C. frozen corn kernels, thawed

¾ tsp. ground cumin

½ tsp. smoked paprika

½ tsp. garlic powder

8 eggs

1 T. skim milk

Black pepper to taste

1 (15 oz.) can "no sodium added" black beans, drained & rinsed

8 (10") whole grain tortillas

1½ C. low-sodium, reduced-fat shredded cheddar cheese

⅔ C. chunky salsa

Heat 1 tablespoon oil in a large nonstick skillet over medium heat. Sauté onion 2 minutes. Stir in corn, cumin, paprika, and garlic powder and cook until tender, 3 or 4 minutes more; set aside.

Whisk together eggs, milk, and pepper. In the same skillet, heat remaining 1 tablespoon oil and add egg mixture, stirring until cooked but still shiny. Remove from heat; stir in the beans and set-aside vegetables. Divide mixture among tortillas, covering half of each. Top evenly with some cheese and salsa. Fold tortillas over filling and press gently. Wipe out skillet and spritz with cooking spray; lightly brown both sides of quesadillas over medium-high heat until cheese melts. Cut into wedges and serve warm.

Make Ahead: Assemble and wrap quesadillas individually, then freeze flat. Store in an airtight container in the freezer. Unwrap and reheat in the microwave, or thaw first and cook in the skillet as directed. ▮

Nutrition

Makes 8 servings
Serving Size: 1 quesadilla

<u>Amount per serving</u>

Calories	325
Total Carbs	31g (10%)
Total Fat	14g (22%)
Sugars	4g
Protein	26g (51%)

Nutrition

Makes 9 servings
Serving Size: 1 mini loaf

<u>Amount per serving</u>

Calories	136
Total Carbs	6g (2%)
Total Fat	7g (10%)
Protein	14g (28%)
Sodium	249mg (10%)

Mini Turkey Loaves

1 T. olive oil

1 C. finely chopped onion

1 red or yellow bell pepper, finely chopped

2 medium carrots, peeled & shredded

1¼ lbs. lean ground turkey

2 egg whites

¼ C. ketchup

1 tsp. dried thyme

½ tsp. dried sage

½ tsp. each salt and black pepper

Preheat the oven to 425°. Grease nine standard muffin cups with cooking spray and set aside.

Heat the oil in a skillet over medium heat and sauté the onion, bell pepper, and carrots until soft, 8 to 10 minutes. Let vegetables cool. In a large bowl, combine the turkey, egg whites, ketchup, thyme, sage, salt, and pepper. Add the vegetables and mix everything together thoroughly. Divide the meat mixture among prepped muffin cups and smooth the top. Bake 20 to 25 minutes or until done. Serve hot with ketchup or whole cranberry sauce, if you'd like. Serving size is one or two loaves, depending on your appetite *(nutrition information based on one).* ▮

Minerals galore, lots of protein, and plenty of A, B, and C vitamins in these little babies!

To Go

Let cooked loaves cool completely and wrap each one in foil. Place in an airtight container and freeze for up to 2 months. To eat, thaw overnight in the refrigerator, unwrap, and reheat in the microwave.

Nutrition

Makes 12 servings
Serving Size: 1 taquito

Amount per serving

Calories	149
Total Carbs	8g (3%)
Total Fat	8g (12%)
Protein	10g (20%)
Sodium	290mg (12%)

Baked Mex-Italian Taquitos

12 oz. sweet Italian chicken sausage, casings removed

1 T. butter

1 C. diced onion

2 or 3 jalapeño peppers, seeded & sliced

1 tsp. minced garlic

6 eggs, lightly beaten

1 T. skim milk

¼ tsp. salt

Black pepper to taste

¾ C. reduced-fat shredded Mexican cheese blend

¼ C. chopped fresh basil

12 (6") corn or flour tortillas

Olive oil

Preheat the oven to 350°. Line a rimmed baking sheet with parchment paper.

Brown the sausage in a skillet over medium heat until crumbly and fully cooked; drain on paper towels and set aside. In the same skillet, melt butter and sauté onion and jalapeños until onion is light golden brown, 3 to 5 minutes. Add the garlic and cook 1 minute more. Whisk together the eggs, milk, salt, and pepper and add to skillet, stirring slowly, until cooked but still shiny. Remove from heat and stir in cheese, basil, and set-aside sausage.

Divide egg mixture among tortillas *(⅓ to ½ cup each)* and roll up tightly. Place on prepped baking sheet, seam side down. Brush with olive oil and bake 20 minutes or until light golden brown and slightly crisp. Serve warm.

Make Ahead: Wrap baked, cooled taquitos in foil and freeze in an airtight container. Before eating, defrost and bake in the oven to crisp up or reheat in the microwave for softer crusts. ∎

Nutrition

Makes 12 servings
Serving Size: 1 egg

Amount per serving

Calories	70
Total Fat	5g (8%)
Sugars	1g
Protein	6g (12%)
Cholesterol	190mg (63%)

Hard-Cooked Oven Eggs

Preheat the oven to 325°. Crumple up some foil in the bottom of each cup in a muffin pan and set one egg in each. Bake on the center rack for 30 minutes. Remove from oven and carefully put each hot egg in ice water. If you plan to use them in a day or two, cool for 10 minutes and then peel off shells; return to water to cool completely. Drain peeled eggs, cover with a damp paper towel, and refrigerate in an airtight container.

If you'd rather use the eggs throughout the week, let them stand in the ice water with shells on until completely cool and then refrigerate. Peel just before using.

Grab a cooked egg or two for an easy breakfast or snack. Add sliced eggs to layered mason jar salads, or mash them up to make your favorite deviled eggs or egg salad with light mayo. ∎

Nutrition

Makes 17 servings
Serving Size: 1 muffin

Amount per serving

Calories	138
Total Carbs	23g (8%)
Total Fat	4g (7%)
Sugars	11g
Cholesterol	21mg (7%)

Banana Walnut Muffins

Preheat the oven to 400°. Grease or line 17 standard muffin cups *(foil liners work best).*

In a large bowl, whisk together ½ C. unsweetened applesauce, 3 T. brown sugar, and ¼ C. stevia baking blend sweetener *(we used Zing)* until smooth. Stir in ½ C. fat-free sour cream. Add 2 eggs and whisk well. Stir in 1 tsp. vanilla and 1½ C. mashed ripe banana. In another bowl, mix ¾ C. each all-purpose flour and whole wheat flour, 1 tsp. baking soda, ½ tsp. each baking powder and salt, and 1 tsp. cinnamon. Gently stir flour mixture into batter. Fold in ¾ C. chopped walnuts. Fill prepared muffin cups ¾ full. Place pan in oven and then reduce heat to 350°. Bake 20 to 24 minutes or until muffins test done with a toothpick. Cool slightly before removing from pan. Store in an airtight container or freeze for up to 1 month. ▌

Add extra flavor, fun, and nutrition to your day with these snack ideas. **Each recipe below makes 4 servings.** ▮

1-Minute Yogurt Pops

Turn a four-pack of fruit-flavored low-fat yogurt cups into frozen pops. Just make a small slit in the lid of each cup with a sharp knife and insert popsicle sticks. Freeze until solid. To eat, separate the cups, run one under warm water, loosen the lid, and remove. Presto! Frozen yogurt popsicles!

Nutrition

Amount per serving

Calories	60	Total Carbs	10g (3%)

4 grams of protein & 15% of your daily calcium needs

Creamy Orange Dip

Stir together ¼ C. light cream cheese spread with ¼ C. low-sugar orange marmalade. Divide among four small to-go cups and bag up some fresh clean strawberries, pineapple chunks, kiwi slices, and/or apples for dipping.

Nutrition

Amount per 2 T. serving

Calories	55	Total Carbs	7g (2%)

Fresh fruit dippers add fiber, crunch & vitamins

Fruit Stacks

Peel and slice
a banana and
kiwifruit into four
even pieces. Dip bananas
in a Fruit Fresh/water mixture
to prevent browning; pat dry. Melt
3 T. semi-sweet chocolate chips and coat
one end of banana pieces; chill in freezer until
set. Slide a strawberry, blueberry, kiwi slice, and
banana onto each skewer. Wrap and chill for 1 or 2 days.

Nutrition

Amount per serving

Calories	81	Total Carbs	16g (5%)

Good dose of Vitamin C plus get-up-and-go energy

Crunchy Apple Wheels

Slice a large Jonagold apple
(or another favorite apple) into
four thin rings and cut out the
core. Spread each ring with
1½ T. reduced-fat creamy
peanut butter and top
with 1 T. chopped pecans,
1 tsp. shredded coconut, and
1 T. raisins or carob chips.

Nutrition

Amount per serving

Calories	306	Total Carbs	35g (12%)

Peanut butter & pecans add a punch of protein

Nutrition

Makes 4 servings
Serving Size: 1 salad

Amount per serving

Calories	281
Total Carbs	18g (6%)
Total Fat	12g (18%)
Sugars	7g
Protein	27g (54%)

Roasted Squash & Pork Salad

¼ C. apple cider vinegar

4 tsp. pure maple syrup

1 tsp. ground allspice

¼ tsp. salt

4 C. each fresh spinach and arugula

2 C. pulled pork *(leftovers work great)*

2 C. roasted butternut squash *(see next page)*

Dark green and orange veggies filled with Vitamins A, C, and K + pork with its B-vitamins = a low-sodium nutrient powerhouse!

Whisk together the vinegar, syrup, allspice, and salt until well blended; set aside. For each salad, layer 2 cups greens, ½ cup pork, and ½ cup roasted squash. Drizzle with some dressing and serve.

To Go: Divide the dressing among four small to-go containers and pack about 2 cups of salad greens into each of four separate containers. In four small microwavable containers, combine ½ cup each pulled pork and roasted squash. Stack all containers in the fridge. Then just grab one of each on your way out the door. To eat, simply reheat the pork and squash in the microwave, dump it on top of the greens, and drizzle with dressing. Toss on some sliced almonds, if you'd like. ∎

Make Ahead

Roast butternut squash or other seasonal vegetables ahead of time and store in the refrigerator to use throughout the week for salads or side dishes. *(Try sweet potatoes, asparagus, broccoli or cauliflower florets, Brussels sprouts, or even jicama.)* Wash and peel the vegetables as needed and cut into uniform pieces. Toss with a bit of olive oil and season ever so lightly with salt and pepper. Spread in a single layer on a foil-lined rimmed baking sheet and roast at 400° *(or 425° if you want more browning)* for 20 to 30 minutes or until fork tender. Refrigerate for up to 5 days.

BBQ Ranch Chicken Wraps

1¼ lbs. chicken breast strips for stir fry

½ C. barbecue sauce, divided

1 C. diced red bell pepper

1 C. frozen corn kernels, thawed

⅓ C. light ranch dressing

1 T. apple cider vinegar

Romaine lettuce

6 pieces whole grain flatbread *(we used Flatout brand)*

Preheat the oven to 425°. Combine chicken and ¼ cup barbecue sauce in a baking dish and bake uncovered for 18 to 20 minutes or until fully cooked. Drain and let cool. Dice the meat into a large bowl and stir in the bell pepper and corn.

Whisk together the ranch dressing, vinegar, and the remaining ¼ cup barbecue sauce in a small bowl. Drizzle about half the dressing mixture over meat mixture and toss well. Cover and refrigerate for up to 3 days. Refrigerate remaining dressing separately.

To assemble, place lettuce leaves on flatbread and spoon a scant 1 cup chicken mixture down the center. Roll up to enclose filling. Serve with remaining dressing as you like.

To Go: Wrap snugly in foil for toting in a cooler. Peel back the foil and dig in. ∎

Nutrition

Makes 6 servings
Serving Size: 1 wrap

<u>Amount per serving</u>

Calories	306
Total Carbs	36g (12%)
Total Fat	7g (10%)
Sugars	12g
Protein	31g (61%)

Nutrition

Makes 1 serving
Serving Size: 1 jar

Amount per serving

Calories	198
Total Carbs	47g (16%)
Sugars	4g
Protein	3g (6%)
Sodium	545mg (23%)

Rice Noodle Soup

Place rice noodle sticks from a 7 oz. package into a plastic bag and break them into smaller pieces; set aside. In each 16 oz. mason jar, combine 2 tsp. low-sodium soy sauce, ½ tsp. each lime juice and chicken bouillon powder, ¼ tsp. each garlic powder and grated gingerroot, and ½ C. each shredded carrot and napa cabbage. Add 12 fresh baby spinach leaves and 1 sliced green onion. Pack a handful of broken noodles into the jar and fasten the lid. Refrigerate for up to 2 days.

Before eating, allow jar to set at room temperature for 15 minutes. Pour about 1½ C. boiling water into the jar to cover noodles; replace lid and let soak 12 minutes or until softened to your liking. Mix soup gently *(jar will be hot!)* and eat from the jar or transfer to a bowl. This fat-free lunch is loaded with Vitamins A, C, and K – and it's so easy! ▮

Nutrition

Makes 25 servings
Serving Size: 1 "bite"

Amount per serving

Calories	105
Total Carbs	12g (4%)
Total Fat	5g (8%)
Sugars	7g
Protein	3g (5%)

No-Bake Energy Bites

Combine 1 C. quick-cooking oats, ⅔ C. shredded sweetened coconut, ½ C. ground flaxseed, ½ C. carob chips, and 1 T. chia seeds in a medium bowl. Stir in ½ C. reduced-fat creamy peanut butter, ⅓ C. honey, and 1 tsp. vanilla until well mixed. Chill for 30 minutes. Shape the mixture into 1″ balls and store in an airtight container in the refrigerator. ▮

A sweet and satisfying low-sodium snack with 16% of your daily fiber needs.

Nutrition

Makes 12 servings
Serving Size: 1 sandwich

Amount per serving

Calories	256
Total Carbs	24g (8%)
Total Fat	9g (14%)
Sodium	519mg (22%)
Cholesterol	206mg (68%)

Breakfast Sandwiches

12 eggs
Black pepper to taste
12 (½ oz.) slices reduced-fat cheddar cheese

12 (⅔ oz.) slices Canadian bacon
12 whole-wheat English muffins, halved

Like a fast-food favorite — but better for you! With 21 grams of protein, one sandwich provides 41% of your daily need for this important building block.

Preheat the oven to 350° and grease 12 standard muffin cups. Crack one egg into each cup and season with pepper. Leave the yolks intact or scramble lightly with a fork. Bake 15 to 18 minutes or until eggs are set. Let cool 30 minutes before gently removing from pan.

To assemble sandwiches, layer one cheese slice, one Canadian bacon slice, and one egg on the bottom half of each muffin; top with remaining muffin halves. Wrap sandwiches in foil or plastic wrap and store in an airtight container. Refrigerate for 1 week or freeze for up to 2 months. ▮

To Go

Toss a refrigerated or frozen sandwich into an insulated lunch container. Unwrap sandwich and cover with a paper towel to reheat in the microwave. If frozen, cook at 50% power about 2 minutes or until heated through, turning halfway through cooking time. Add some zip with mustard or pesto, if you'd like.

Index